Granny Glen's Poems

Glen Hughes

ISBN: 978-1-9999557-6-2

Illustrations by Anna Landmane and Stafford Publishers

with colour work by Stafford Publishers

First published by Stafford Publishers 2019

Stafford Publishers

www.staffordpublishers.com

To my grandchildren

all of them.

Contents

Granny Glen's Poems

Clouds

At the top of the world's highest mountain

Sits a giant as big as can be.

What`s he doing up there? You may ask me.

Well he`s brewing a big pot of tea.

His kettle is made out of copper

Which he polishes all of the time

For the top of a mountain is dusty,

It`s hard work to give it a shine.

But you`ll know when the kettle is boiling

As the steam will fill up the sky,

And puffs of fluffy, white steam clouds

Will drift over, passing by.

Stars

The stars are all kisses

Each sent from above

To remind us at night time

God sends us his love.

Thunder

If the giant in the sky gets a fly in his eye

It makes it hard to see.

He may stumble and fall to the ground with a call!

As he lands on his giant sized knee!

The rumbling sound will be heard all around,

Over miles, over earth, sand and sea.

He`ll roll over, he`ll roll under,

And we`ll think that it`s thunder,

But it`s just the giants big, bad knee!

The Milky Way and Fog

Up above beyond the stars,

Way past Venus, Mercury and Mars,

There`s a giant race track

Built for giant sized cars!

Earth is such a way away

Said Giant B to Giant A.

If we could build a road my friend

Along of which we could send

Giants speeding in their racing cars

Whizzing round and round the stars!

Oh! Yes said Giant A to B

A giant race track I can see

Would be an awful lot of fun.

And so! The building work begun

Excitement grew up in the place

Where giants live in outer space.

And very soon the track was ready,

Cars on the start line waiting steady.

Chequered flag was raised up high

To start that first race in the sky.

Giant bonnets, giant bumpers,

Giant drivers in giant jumpers

Sat behind their steering wheel

Round the corners tyres squeal!

Engines roaring, off they go,

Where`s the finish? I don`t know!

The tracks so big that I can`t see

Said Giant A to Giant B.

The track is called The Milky Way

And can be seen, or so they say,

By us, on nights` the sky is clear,

On summer nights it seems so near

But `tis so far, far away.

Looks wonderful! The Milky Way!

But round and round the giant cars go

So very fast and never slow!

They`re going still and never stop,

Well, just for fuel, and a lollipop!

And though the Earth`s so far away

There are some days I have to say

The dust kicked up from all this motion

Falls to Earth causing great commotion!

Through fog we fail to find our way

And in our homes we have to stay!

A blocked sink

There`s something lurking in the kitchen sink.

An evil smelling brew

Fermenting in the U-bend.

Can you smell it too?

There`s rumblings in the kitchen pipes.

The pressures building high!

I`d stand well back if I were you,

Don`t bother asking why!

Look out there! Well I warned you.

What a hideous stink!

I told you there was something

Lurking in the kitchen sink.

Sun and Moon

There`s a trillion, billion light bulbs making up the sun,

And a giant electrician looks after each and every one.

He ensures they`re bright and shiny every single day,

Testing them, and dusting them so that`s the way they`ll stay.

He carries out inspections at night time with great care,

But now and then he drops one, creating solar flare!

The bulbs at night are all switched off, save but for a few,

As the giant electrician knows he has a job to do.

He needs a little light to see his way around,

So any bulbs a dimming can easily be found.

Each night he carries with him a great big giant sack

To carry home the old bulbs slung upon his back.

He takes them to his work shop, to see what he can do,

And if he can`t repair them he orders some brand new.

If you`ve ever been awake at night and peeped up at the moon,

You`ll know that he is working to restore full power real soon!

The dim glow from the brand new bulbs will be seeping from his sack

As he lifts it up to reach right in, see his big face smiling back.

His gentle, giant digits pick out new bulbs, one by one

Expertly replacing them into a socket in the sun.

So, just as day is dawning and it`s time for us to rise

We can see the sun shine brightly up above us in the skies!

Gravity

Gregory Gilmore Goggins is a friendly sort of guy,

He`s built of giant proportions, miles wide and broad and high!

He has an occupation where he lives in outer space

And that`s to keep Earth turning at just the perfect pace.

Gregory Gilmore Goggins works hard all night and day,

He carries out his work in a conscientious way.

Gregory Gilmore Goggins has hands the size of France

And arms as strong as big, blue whales, you can see at just a glance

He`s built for work upon this scale, his employment`s not by chance!

There`s a planetary system of cogs and wheels and gears,

And Gregory Gilmore Goggins has kept it running well for years.

He turns a handle that turns the sun that turns the planets around,

And all of this so we are sure to stick upon the ground!

Beacon Park Beetle

I'm a lovely little beetle

And I live in Beacon Park,

But you won't have seen me out about

Cause I'm out just after dark.

I'm a black and shiny beetle

With six short legs, I scurry.

I burrow down beneath the earth

Always busy, in a hurry!

I'm a friendly little beetle

And I like to share my lunch

With worms and other bugs around

Dead leaves we love to munch!

To a cheery little beetle

Park Ranger's not unkind

No toxic sprays used around here

Organics all you'll find.

I'm a thankful little beetle

For the park's a place to stay

The Bug Hotel has a room for all

Where I meet my friends to play.

Trolls!

Beware! Beware! There`s a troll out there!

You may think you`re alone on a walk in the wood

But the poke in your back lets you know that there could

At the side of a rock or behind a big tree,

Be a naughty Troll just as bold as can be!

Waiting for his chance to jump out on folk

For there`s nothing so good as a prank or a joke!

He`ll tap on your shoulder and pull on your hair

If you`re nervous at all he can give you a scare!

But it`s mischief he`s making, just fooling around.

When he`s had all his fun he`ll go back underground.

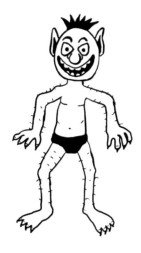

Up in the night

There`s something creeping round the bedroom.

In the dark it`s hard to see.

Burglar or spectre what ever could it be?

I must protect my husband dear!

So moving very slow

I reach out for a missile, something I can throw.

There`s a copy of a gardening book right here beside the bed.

I lift and aim the weighty tome

And hit it round the head!

The apparition yells and groans, a most unearthly sound.

As I pull upon the light switch

See my husband on the ground!

Oh! Dear! So it got you then despite my daring efforts,

If I hadn`t fought so bravely your injuries would be worse.

What was that he muttered?

It sounded like a curse!

Well how ungrateful can you be!

Next time just you wait!

When I see a ghost come creeping in

I`ll leave you to your fate!

Up in the night again!

Nigel`s in a hurry.

Where`s he off to at that speed?

I think he has to satisfy

His bi-nocturnal need.

Now he`s looking worried,

There`s a puddle on the floor.

He`s going to have to get the mop

And clean it up once more!

Noises in the night

There`s a rumbling in the water pipes,

It`s creating quite a racket!

We`ll have to call the plumber in

It`s going to cost a packet!

Griff

You`ll see him on his scooter,

Whizzing by real fast.

He `outa have a hooter

To toot as he goes past.

But he likes to take you unaware,

Speeding up behind,

Racing past without a care

Watch him bump and grind

Past people, pushchairs, cars, `n all

Red Ensign flag a flying,

And as he goes you`ll hear him call,

"Can`t catch me! No point trying!"

Aunty Carol

Aunty Carol has big ears,

They make her look quite funny.

There`s no one else with ears so big

Apart from my pet bunny!

Aunty Carol has big ears.

She wears them on her head.

I wonder if she takes them off

Before she goes to bed?

Uncle Rob

Uncle Rob`s a sailor man,

He travels near and far.

He stands upon the bridge all day,

At night he`s in the bar!

Uncle Rob`s a sailor man,

He`s taking me to sea.

He`ll teach me everything he knows,

So a sailor man I`ll be!

Richard has short legs

Richards' legs are short and mean,

With knobbly knees a knocking!

In summer when he dons his shorts

The sight of them is shocking!

Grandad`s Teeth - By a boy aged one year

Grandad has false teeth.

I think they`re really cool.

I hope that I can have a set

Before I go to school!

Diamonds

Have you ever wondered what happens to your teeth
When they're pushed out by the bigger ones growing
underneath?
And you place them very carefully `neath the pillow on your bed,
But when, next day, you look and find a coin is there instead!
It`s because you`ve had a visit in the middle of the night
From a troop of tiny people when your eyes were closed real
tight.
They are fairies on a mission to collect all that they can,
And when their sacks are full of teeth they load them in a van,
Then take them off to Fairy Land to a work shop where they`ll
toil
As hard as any fairy can that lives upon this soil!
They cut them into pretty shapes and rub them with a duster,
Plus, a little magic fairy spit gives them incandescent lustre!
Then their dainty fairy fingers fix them to the top
Of every fairy magic wand existing in that shop!
If any are left over, cause they`re faulty (or just spare),
They take them to a secret place (though faults are very rare),
And they put them in a storage space a short way underground
Letting unsuspecting humans think it's diamonds they have
found!

Getting Old

I`m searching for my glasses,

I`m sure I left them here.

The worlds a very misty place

Without my optic gear!

Just a day without them

Fills my heart with dread.

What a silly buffer!

They`re right here on my head!

In Praise of Fish!

You wanted a poem exalting the fish,

The fish that swim in the sea.

So an ode I have written in praise of the catch

Cause they taste as good as can be!

Covered in scales, shiny and bright,

They swim with the greatest of ease.

But gutted and grilled and put on a plate

Go well with chips and green peas!

Rabbits Revenge!

I sit and watch and wait and stare

All you humans unaware

Of watching eyes and things they see

You pass me by, no thought for me.

Sweeping changes (and sometimes small),

Not conscious it affects us all!

You put in paths and take down trees.

Mother Nature`s on her knees!

But in this green and pretty place

Time`s the winner of the race.

You may rule when the sun is high,

Bright and shining in the sky.

But then at night when the sun is down

You humans leave behind your crown,

And out in force the rabbits come,

Flopsy, Mopsy and Peter Bun!

Devouring the plants you planted in the park!

Yes! Rabbits rule round here after dark!

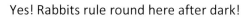

Sean The Leprechaun

He came right out of nowhere in a suit of emerald green.

He was the very smallest man that I had ever seen.

Black, shiny, shoes upon his feet, striped stockings to his knees.

An eerie mist wound round his whole, blown in upon a breeze.

He raised his hat politely, wished me well this early morn,

And told me "I`m a leprechaun known locally as Sean!"

"Well! Sean the leprechaun!" I replied with a wily smile,

"I`m a visitor to this home of yours, this splendid Emerald Isle!"

I was hoping he may grant a wish upon this day to me,

A rainbows end and a treasure trove was what I`d hoped to see.

The hoard they say`s enormous, each coin earned fair and square

By the leprechauns of Ireland who save and hide it there.

But he knew what I was thinking, he`d been asked as much before

And warned me not to make my wish until I was quite sure!

For `tis leprechaun gold, not human! And one touch of human hand

Transforms it into tiny grains of soft and golden sand!

Many have been fooled this way, not heeding my advice,

They should have thought of things worthwhile, could have thought of something nice,

Warm sunny days, blue skies above, this and so much more!

But greed instead takes over and it`s filling up our shore!

They think they know much better than old Sean the leprechaun

And have been here in their thousands every evening, night and morn.

Each eager for a crock of gold, now a million miles of sand!

And the only thing it`s good for`s filling gap twixt sea and land!

The Runaway Haggis

Christmas was gone and Hogmanay too,

Twenty-fifth of the month, Burns Night was due.

`Ma in her kitchen was stuffing the Beast,

A Haggis so big we were promised a feast!

Disaster then struck as `Ma lost her grip

And it sailed `cross the room like a mighty airship!

It bounced off the table and on to the floor

Just as Jim arrived home and opened the door!

It flew passed Jim and sleeping dog Buster.

"After it Jim!" cried `Ma in a fluster.

Buster and Jim were joined by young Bill,

Giving chase as it bounded away down the hill!

Jock stood alone at his green, garden gate

As the Haggis rushed by at a hell of a rate!

Jock leapt in the air and over that barrier

Joining Jim with the speed of a sparrow hawk harrier!

Janet was out hanging washing to dry

When the haggis went hurrying, scurrying by!

She picked up her skirts and joined in the chase.

By now the whole village was on to the case!

Careering along, crashing through heather,

Over tussock and hillock like wild, winter weather!

It tumbled and tossed itself all around.

A terrible pace travelling over the ground!

It forged on ahead making way over moor,

Rapidly nearing the cliff and the shore!

Pitched over the cliff, splashed into the sea!

Now all we have left is tatties for tea!

Cheers! I`ll Have a Gin!

Hoorah! For the good gin and tonic!

The most refreshing of drink.

See the bubbles that rise in the glasses,

Then together those tumblers chink!

Hoorah! For the juniper bushes!

Best served with ice and a slice.

For a wine or a beer may be pleasant,

But a gin is ever so nice!

What If...

If Douglas Adams was quite right

And the world was run by mice,

Would it matter if they`re black or white

As long as they were nice?

And if the tortoise turning us was moving fast or slow

Would it matter much to all of us?

As long as we all know

That turning will continue by this giant beast

Who doesn`t seem to mind the fact

In the very least!

What if the world was really flat?

And the moon was made of cheese,

And mountain tops were ice-cream

On the caps of giants' knees!

His hands would be great continents,

His feet two more land masses,

His ears a giant tunnel

Through which a fast train passes

Taking all the people on a trip down to his chest

To eat the lemon sherbet that he spilled inside his vest!

We wouldn`t care about a thing
Except for one another.
One big happy family,
Each a sister or a brother.
Under clouds of candyfloss
We`d swim in lakes of toffee,
Round islands made of apple pie
And rivers run with coffee!

Each day we`d wake up feeling glad
We`d slept well through the night,
And think the great, big brandy ball
A wondrous, marvellous sight!

Winter Storms

Grandpa Globbit despite his age was really rather fast,

Charging round the cosmos at a speed that`s unsurpassed

By all his family elders, and the young `uns too!

No one could keep up with him as he charged across the blue!

Grandpa Globbit galloped around the stars at night.

From Earth he could be spotted as a moving, bright red light.
In a net he`d try to catch space rockets wearing nothing but his vest!

But he never caught a single one, just a cold upon his chest!

His coughing and his wheezing meant Grandma Globbit didn`t sleep.
The rush of air and roaring sound even stopped her counting sheep!
The whistling and the whooshing weighed the atmosphere right down,
Sending streams of moving air to Earth jetting round and round!

And so on Earth the wind whipped up the waves upon the sea!
It sent dried leaves from the trees in a whirling, wild frenzy!
Roof top tiles and chimney pots came crashing to the ground!
And Grandpa Globbits grunts and roars blotted out all other sound!

Grandpa Globbits head, despite his chill, felt somewhat rather hot!
Breathing hard because his nose was very full of snot!
When a terrible, tickle tingled through his nasal tubes!
Where his sinuses were all blocked up with the excess lubes!

Then that tickling sensation grew ever so much worse.

Had breathing been an option we`d have certainly heard him curse!

But instead, the tickle moved around inside his head!

Giving Grandpa cause to rise up fast from off his bed!

There he stood with muscles tensed about to blow!

What happened next I think you all will know!

Throwing down his head he sneezed between his feet!

And here on Earth we all got soaked in sleet!